Sales Representative Agreements

Explanations of Terms, Options and Sample Rep Contracts

Robert Belt
Lawrence Harte

ALTHOS

Althos Publishing
Fuquay-Varina, NC 27526 USA
Telephone: 1-800-227-9681
Fax: 1-919-557-2261
email: info@althos.com
web: www.Althos.com

Althos

Copyright © 2008 By Althos Publishing
First Printing

Printed and Bound by Lightning Source, TN.

International Standard Book Number: 1-932813-69-1

About the Authors

 Mr. Belt is a new product business development, marketing and sales expert for communications products. Robert specializes in assisting international and OEM companies in finding, qualifying, establishing meetings, defining product requirements, negotiation of sales contracts and follow-up customer communication. He has more than 20 years of experience in product definition, engineering specification, design and contract negotiation for non-standard products. Mr. Belt has defined and located for strategic partnering, initiated discussions for technology partnering and drafted alliance agreements. Robert's clients have included Alps, Motorola, Nokia, Wavetek, Norand, Trimble, Mitsubishi, Panasonic, Fujitsu, Uniden, NEC, Qualcomm, Novatel, JRC, Apple, Omnipoint, NYNEX, Bell Atlantic, SONY and hundreds of other companies.

 Mr. Harte is the president of Althos, an expert information provider which researches, trains, and publishes on technology and business industries. He has over 29 years of technology analysis, development, implementation, and business management experience. Mr. Harte has worked for leading companies including Ericsson/General Electric, Audiovox/Toshiba and Westinghouse and has consulted for hundreds of other companies. Mr. Harte continually researches, analyzes, and tests new communication technologies, applications, and services. He has authored over 80 books on telecommunications technologies and business systems covering topics such as mobile telephone systems, data communications, voice over data networks, broadband, prepaid services, billing systems, sales, and Internet marketing. Mr. Harte holds many degrees and certificates including an Executive MBA from Wake Forest University (1995) and a BSET from the University of the State of New York, (1990).

Table of Contents

Sales Representative

A sales representative is a person who performs sales functions for one or more companies. Companies use sales representatives to sell products and services in defined geographic areas to certain types of customers.

Sales representative agreements define the working relationship between the sales representative and the company. The terms in these agreements define and clarify expectations between the company and the sales representative. Good sales representative agreements, which are understood by both parties, can lead to a much better relationship and less conflicts.

Sales representative agreements can range from short 1 to 2 page agreements to long detailed contracts. Sales representative agreements can be linked to other documents (such as travel policies) to reduce the length and complexity of the agreement.

While sales representative agreements define specific requirements on the relationship between a sales representative and a company, there is more to a sales representative agreement than the specific terms, responsibilities and compensation plans.

Sales representative agreements are typically created as a result of a need to meet sales objectives. The process of how to use sales departments and sales representatives is defined in a sales plan.

Sales Objectives

Sales objectives are statements that identify targets that should be achieved through sales efforts that may include items such as revenue, new customer types, new channel types, or profit margins. Sales targets are quantities of companies, products or revenue values that are assigned to be achieved or used to develop a list of actions to achieve them. Sales targets may be associated with a commission structure or bonus system to help motivate and reward people for helping to achieve sales objectives.

Revenue Targets

Revenue targets are sales values that desired along with the associated time periods which the sales should be achieved. Revenue targets may defied in gross sales or net sales amounts. Examples of revenue targets include $1.2 million in sales per year or $100,000 per month.

Product Types

Product types are the defining of products into groups that are based on characteristics such as size, function, brand, durability, or cost. Examples of product type categories include consumer, original equipment manufacturer (OEM), industrial and military. While it is desirable that product types are unique, in practice, some product types may overlap.

Consumer products are devices or items that are designed to appeal to a wide range of customer types. Consumer products may be sold in high-quantity to mass market outlets (such as retail store chains). The process of selling consumer products can range from dealing with individual retailers or consumers to dealing with corporate buyers for large companies who can specify complicated support requirements.

OEM products are objects or assemblies that are designed, modified or labeled so they can be sold by other companies under their brands. OEM product sales tends to be a more complicated than selling other products due to the need for technical and product design specifications.

Industrial products are devices or materials that are purchased or used by companies that produce or manufacture products or services. Industrial products are designed to meet strong reliability and durability specifications. Selling industrial products can require technical understanding (such as a sales engineer) or skills that relate to the goods or products that are being sold.

Military products are devices or services that are purchased or used by military organizations. Military products are commonly designed to meet detailed requirements specifications such as military specifications (Mil Specs), which can have extreme operational performance and durability requirements. Selling military products and services may involve responding to lengthy bids issued by a government agency. A trend that began in the 1990s was the moving away from Mil Spec requirements towards standard market specifications in an attempt to reduce price and lead time while increasing the number of available suppliers.

Product type sales objectives can be used to help a company to evolve or develop business in specific areas. For example, a company may desire to increase its production volume by expanding its product lines from industrial to consumer. Sales people may be provided with added incentives (such as increased commissions, stipends, or spiffs) for selling new types of products. Approved products to sell may be included in an appendix.

Figure 1.1 shows a sample of a sales plan that sets targets consumer, military and industrial product type categories. This example also shows that product type targets can have different categories such as retail entry (prestige brand) and premium (gold brand).

Product Type	Target
Consumer	180,000 units Prestige Brand 80,000 units Gold Brand
Military	24,000 units
Industrial	42,000 units Metals 16,000 units - Plastics

Figure 1.1, Sample Sales Product Objectives

Channel Types

A channel type is a set of characteristics associated with how products are transferred from the manufacturer or source of the products to the customers who use or consume them. Examples of channel types include direct, wholesale, distributor and retail.

A direct sales channel uses employees or company controlled systems that directly promote and communicate with the buyers of products or services. Direct sales channels typically consume large quantities of standard products.

Indirect sales channel is the use of other people or companies (such as sales representatives) to promote or communicate with buyers of products or services. Indirect sales channels may include sales representatives who can cost effectively sell related types of products or services.

Wholesale sales channels are companies that purchase large quantities of products that they resell to distributors or retailers. Wholesale channels may be used to reduce the number of orders and to guarantee sales revenue for products or services.

Distributor sales channels provide products or services to retailers. Distributors directly interact with the retailers to ensure products are stocked and sold. A company may have multiple distributors and each distributor may be assigned to specific geographic regions.

Retail sales channels are stores or online merchants that sell products directly to consumer. Retail sales channels often have trained salespeople that can explain and promote similar types of products and services. For companies that use distributors, product requests from retail stores are transferred to the appropriate distributor.

Using multiple sales and distribution channels can result in conflicts due to channel cannibalization. Channel cannibalization is the consumption or decrease in sales of an existing product or service as a result of introducing or providing another product or service. An example of channel cannibalization is selling direct to businesses or customers can cause conflict with other channels. To overcome the potential conflicts from competing channels, sales channels may be given exclusivity or price protection in specific areas.

Profit Margins

Profit margin is the percentage of the revenue generated from sales that is above the total costs of selling or providing products and services. Companies that desire to maximize the profit margin may reward sales representatives for achieving the highest profit margin.

Sales representatives may not know which products have the highest profit margins and companies may not want to provide product cost information. If achieving profit margin is an objective, profit margin should be defined, as it may be possible to allocate other costs into the profit margin equation (such as overhead) resulting in unexpected changes in sales commissions.

Sales Plan

A sales plan contains the objectives of the sales process, the responsibilities and incentives of those involved in the sales process, and the resources that will be available or used for the sales process. The sales plan usually includes objectives (sales targets), assigned sales representatives, what products they are authorized to sell, list of sales roles, responsibilities, and territories. A sales plan (written or unwritten) is commonly used as a basis for defining and negotiating the terms of sales representative agreements.

Sales Territory

Sales territories are regions or geographic boundaries that are assigned to salespeople or sales departments. Sales territories may be referenced to regions such as countries, states, counties or areas on maps. Some of the common divisions of global geographic regions include continents and areas within continents divided by geographic boundaries (such as east or west of the Mississippi River).

Figure 1.2 shows a sample listing of sales regions and sales people who are assigned to them. This table shows a company that has divided the world into 6 geographic regions. One of these regions is rest of world (ROW) which is the assignment of geographic areas that are outside other assigned territories.

Sales Region	Sales Representative
Eastern USA	Bob Smith
Western USA	Jane Doe
Europe	Peter Frank
Caribbean	Tamara Belo
Gulf Cooperation Council (GCC)	Ahmad Salah
South Asian Association for Regional Cooperation (SAARC)	Sue Sharp
Central and Latin America (CALEA)	Jose Gonzalez
Rest of World (ROW)	James Globe

Figure 1.2, Sample Sales Territory Assignments

Authorized Products

Authorized products are a list of products or services that a person or company is authorized to sell. The products that sales representatives may be authorized to sell might be limited certain product lines or even specific products. These may be identified in the agreement or as an appendix that is attached to the agreement.

Authorized products may be identified by product groups or even product numbers. Product groups or product families share common characteristics (such as the same electronic assemblies). They may be assigned a group name.

Authorized products may also be defined by a type of operation or technology that the products use. For example, a sales representative may be authorized to sell mobile telephones that use a specific type of technology or communication capability.

Exclusivity

Exclusivity is the assignment of rights to a single person or company. Exclusivity provides a sales representative with an incentive to invest in sales efforts, as they are not concerned about the potential loss of sales due to competing sales channels. Exclusivity may be assigned for a product, customer or geographic region.

When exclusivity is provided, it typically includes conditions or performance requirements to maintain exclusivity. Exclusivity terms may be subject to review and modification and may have renewal options.

Account Types

Account types are the defining of customer accounts into groups that are based on characteristics such as location, distribution function and the products that they carry. Examples of account types include retail, distributor, original equipment manufacturer (OEM), value-added reseller (VAR), and house accounts. While it is desirable that account types are unique, in practice, some account types may overlap. Sales representatives may be assigned to different types of accounts.

Retail Account

Retail accounts are customers that own or operate stores or online businesses that sell products directly to consumers. Retail account sales support needs may include product training, point of sale materials and displays and checking and restocking of inventory.

Distributor Accounts

Distributor accounts are companies or organizations that supply products or services to retailers. Distributor account sales support needs may include order management, order tracking and the supply of product media and literature.

OEM Account

Original equipment manufacturer accounts are companies or organizations that provide a product, which uses components, assemblies or completed products that are produced for their customers. OEM account sales support needs may include technical support, design services and skilled negotiations. When a company designs and produces a product for another company, they are called an original design manufacturer (ODM).

VAR Account

Value added reseller accounts are companies or organizations that sell products or services by enhancing (adding value) to products or services from other companies. VAR account sales representative support needs may include the ability to access and communicate with technical staff and providing design details of products and services.

House Account

A house account is a customer account that is directly managed by the company that produces or provides the products or services. Some companies don't allow a house account as they do not have direct sales staff or they prefer to avoid conflict with other types of sales channels. When a company does not have house accounts, all the sales leads that are received are forwarded to appropriate sales representatives or organizations.

Figure 1.3 shows how a sales plan may define different types of accounts and some of their sales support requirements. Retail accounts may require some product feature and operation training along with inventory checking and restocking. Distributor and wholesale account types may require continued monitoring and tracking of orders. OEM and VAR accounts may require technical sales support capabilities.

Account Type	Sales Support Requirements
Retail	Product training, inventory checking and restocking
Distributor/Wholesale	Order management and order tracking
OEM/VAR	Technical support, design services and skilled negotiations

Figure 1.3, Sample Account Type Support Requirements

Assignment Rights

Assignment rights are the authorization to allow some or all of the claims, rights, interest or property in an agreement to be transferred to another person or company.

Sales representatives may employ other people such as administrators or other salespeople to assist in their sales assignments. When sales representatives use direct employees to perform actions defined by the sales representative agreement, these people may be also bound under the terms of the agreement.

In some cases, sales representatives may recruit or work with other sales representatives. These people that manage other sales representatives or sales representative groups are called super representatives (super reps).

Sales Commissions

A sales commission is a value assigned or awarded to a salesperson or other entity for obtaining or servicing a customer. The sales commission is typically paid at sometime after a sale to a customer is completed. Commissions may be paid in cash or other assets such as product samples (e.g. free car). Sales commission rates can range from simple straight (fixed) commission that is a % of sales to complex commission schedules with overrides and bonuses.

Sales Commission Schedule

A sales commission schedule is an itemized list or table that provides commission levels that are paid for the sales of products or services that occur in specific ranges or categories.

Sales commission rates generally go down as sales go up. The more a sales person sells, the smaller the amount of commission that is paid for the increased amounts. It is structured this way to help allow companies to offer products and services at competitive prices as the sales volumes increase.

Commission amounts are typically calculated and accumulated for each level (or band) they are associated with. For example, a commission schedule that pays 6% for the first $500,000 in sales and 5% for $500,000 to $1,000,000 in sales would pay $55,000 ($30,000 + $25,000) in commission for $1,000,000 sales revenue.

Some companies may use inverted commission schedules (higher commissions with higher sales levels) to help motivate sales people to sell larger amounts during specific time periods. This may be done in markets where there is a limited product lifecycle.

Figure 1.4 shows a sample sales commission schedule. This table shows that a sales person will receive 6% for sales up to $500,000 over a 1-year period. As the annual sales volume increases, the sales commission decreases. The commission rate is exclusively paid for each sales level and combined to determine the sales commission.

Sales Volume (yearly)	Commission Rate
Up to $500,000	6%
$500,000 to $1,000,000	5%
$1,000,001 to $1,999,999	4%
$2,000,000 and over	3%

Example: Sales of $3,000,000 in a year would pay a commission of $125,000 ($30,000 + $25,000 + $40,000 + $30,000).

Figure 1.4, Sample Sales Commission Schedule

Sales commission may be calculated on various types of sales measurements including product quantity sales, gross sales and net sales amounts. The definition of gross and net sales can vary so they may be defined and included in the sales representative agreement.

Gross Sales

Gross sales are the total recorded revenue for products or services (not including shipping cost). Gross sales may be defined in agreements as the total amount of invoices before applying discounts, allowances, or returns.

Net Sales

Net sales are the recorded revenue for products or services less discounts, allowances, or returns. Some net sales deductions may include freight, transaction fees, marketing costs, and catalog management fees.

Returns and Allowances

Returns and allowances are amounts of value that are given to offset a price or previously agreed upon term. Commissions that were paid on returned products are usually deducted from the next commission payment.

Sales rep may be asked to assist in collection of invoices. This is because the sales representative may have a relationship with the customer who can assist in the communication and motivation of customers to pay their bills.

Royalties and Licensing Fees

Royalties are compensation for the assignment or use of intellectual property rights. License fees are an amount charged or assigned to an account for the authorization to use a product, service, or asset. License fees can be a fixed fee, percentage of sales, or a combination of the two. Sales representatives may be awarded bonuses or percentages of royalties or license fees they obtain for the company using a different commission or sales commission rate or plan.

Sales Bonuses

Sales bonuses are additional sales incentives that are provided when some criteria are achieved. An example of a sales bonus is the paying of an additional $1,000 is sales commission for the obtaining of a new corporate sales customer.

Bonuses may also be in the form of a sales spiff, which provides marketing incentives from one company directly to sales representatives of another company (usually a retail sales company). Spiffs are often used to focus sales representatives or sales agents on demonstrating and giving preference to products or services from a specific manufacturer.

Override Commissions

An override commission is a value that is assigned or awarded to people or companies on products or services that are paid in addition to or instead of other commissions. An example of an override commission is a sales percentage that is paid to a division leader for all the products that are sold in their department regardless of who sold the products or services.

Barters

Barter is an exchange of items, media or services that are used as value instead of the use of money. An example of a barter sale is the providing of a new car in exchange of advertising time on a radio or television program.

Because barters may not result in any cash or monetary sales, sales commission may not be able to be calculated even though a sale is completed. While the sales representative may not qualify for commissions on barter exchanges, the company may still pay commissions or provide added incentives. While bartering may not involve cash transfers, they may be subject to tax assessments.

Payment Schedule

A payment schedule is an itemized list or table that provides payment amounts that is provided when specific actions or payments will be processed. Payment schedules that may apply to sales representative agreements include sales commissions, retainers, draws and expenses.

Expenses

Expenses are the costs that occur as a result of creation of revenue or performance of an action. Sales representatives may receive compensation for some of the expenses they incur on behalf of their relationship with the company. For example, a sales representative may attend a trade show at the request of the company. As a result of this request, the company may pay for some or all of the travel expenses.

Getting reimbursed for expenses usually requires authorization. Expense authorization may be assigned (within limits) or it may require approval from the company each time an expense occurs. The expense approval process may be a combination of expense filing requirements (expense reports) along with manager approvals.

Expense Allowances

Expense allowances are values that are pre-assigned for expense categories that can be charged without budgeting or authorization. An example of an expense allowance is the authorization to receive a per diem (per day) rate is the amount of value or charges that may be provided per day when traveling on behalf of the company.

Travel Expenses

Travel expenses are costs incurred during travel between locations. Travel expenses may include transportation ticket costs (plane, train, taxi), leased vehicle cost, automobile usage (mileage), and meals that occur during travel. To be reimbursed for travel expenses, the sales representative may have to follow established travel policies.

To get reimbursed for travel expenses, employees and sales representatives may be required to conform to travel policies. Travel policies are a set of rules or guidelines that define acceptable types of travel costs and how the travel should be booked, paid for, and processed. This can include such polices as acceptable method of travel (car, train, plane, bus), acceptable class of travel (coach, business class, first class), acceptable class of car rental (premium, mid-size, economy), acceptable lodging options (premium, mid-tier business hotel, economy motel), acceptable meal amount, and acceptable travel expenses (dry cleaning, room service, tipping, in—room movies, high speed internet connections, cancellation fees, booking fees, taxis, entertainment).

Some companies do allow a 5% to 10% handling fee for processing expense reports. This is supposed to compensate for the time required to complete and file expense reports along with the use of personal finances, which may be used to pay for expenses before they are reimbursed from the company.

Combined business and personal travel may be allowed for certain types of travel. An example would be a convention in a popular tourist destination is scheduled for Monday through Wednesday. It may be permissible for the sales representatives to arrive on Saturday for relaxation time before the convention. The expenses may be apportioned appropriately.

Travel Arrangements

Travel arrangements are the reserving or booking of travel related activities such as buying airline tickets, reserving hotels or booking car rentals. Sales representatives may be required to use approved travels agents or specific types of travel related companies.

Expense Report

An expense report is a form or document that identifies, organizes and totals expenses for an employee, contractor or company. A sales representative may be required to submit expense reports within a defined time period (such as within 1 month).

Entertainment Expenses

An entertainment expense is a fee or assessment that occurs as a result of activities that are performed to help motivate or assist in the development of business or project related activities. An example of an entertainment expense is a dinner meeting or trip for a customer or potential customer, which is paid for by the company. Entertainment expenses may require approval.

Some entertainment expenses may be negotiable on an individual basis. For example, a sales representative may be presented with a key opportunity to meet with a potential client and decide to pay for the expense. This expense may be submitted to the company for approval and payment after the expense has occurred. While the sales representative is not guaranteed payment for the expense by the company, if their performance and sales record is good, the company may pay the expense.

Other types of entertainment that may be acceptable as part of a sales representative agreement include sporting expenses such as skybox rental, tickets for theater events and other entertainment functions that may be helpful to business relationships.

Promotional Items

A promotional item is an object or service that is given to a person or company to help build awareness, interest or provide convenient contact information. Examples of promotional items include pens, coffee mugs, or memory sticks.

Sales representatives may be given allowances for promotional items that they can give to customers and prospects. The amount may be limited based on the levels of sales or other qualifications. Some sales representative may share the expense of promotional items.

Office Expenses

Office expenses are the fee or assessments that occur as a result purchasing or using equipment or services for office activities. Examples of office expenses include administrative software, space rental, equipment rental, paper supplies and telephone services. Sales representatives may receive allowances for office expenses such as mobile phone, office supplies and business cards. The amount of reimbursement for sales expenses may be prorated for shared business and personal expenses (such as home office).

Expense Advances

Expense advances are the providing of cash or assets that will be used for the purchase of products or services in advance of when the products or services will be provided. Advance types include cash advances and travel advances. Sales representatives may be provided advances or retainers. Advances may be in the form of prepaid expenses such as airline tickets.

Company Policies

Company policies are a set of rules or guidelines that define acceptable and/or unacceptable types of activities and actions that may be performed by employees, contractors or other people who work with the company. Company policies range from a code of conduct (general behavior policies) to acceptable use policies.

Sales representative agreements may reference policy documents. However, it is possible that the companies do not provide copies of these documents with the sales representative agreements.

Code of Conduct

A code of conduct is a set of rules or guidelines that define how people or companies should act. A code of conduct may be specified as part of an agreement to help ensure those employees, sales representatives and/or contractors behave in a consistent and acceptable way as part of the terms of their agreement.

Conflict of Interest

A conflict of interest is situation where a person or a company has responsibilities, agreements or personal interest to perform actions that could limit, reduce or harm their ability to perform actions for another person or company.

Conflicts of interest could include such things as representing two similar products by different manufacturers in the same territory and creating a product for sale similar to a product they are representing.

Privacy Policy

A privacy policy is the self-proclaimed rules a receiver of information claims to follow when a customer or visitor sends or provides information. Privacy policy rules typically state how the information may be used and to whom the information may be distributed.

Gift Policy

Gifts are the providing of an item or service to a person or company without requiring direct compensation or reward from the recipient. Gifts may be given to help or encourage communication with a potential customer or person. Companies may have gift policies that define if and how gifts may be given or received. An example of a gift is a coffee mug that contains the web address of a company.

Acceptable Use Policy (AUP)

An acceptable use policy is the rules and requirements for the use of equipment and services by a person, company or agency. AUPs typically restrict the use of equipment and services to actions that are related to the performance of job duties.

Sales Lists

A sales list is a group of contacts that have a common set of characteristics such as customers that have already purchased products or are a group of contacts that are potential customers (sales prospects). Sales lists are typically owned and managed by the company that uses them.

List Ownership

List ownership is the person or company who has the rights to use, maintain or sell lists. Lists are commonly owned by the company that retains the sales representative. However, some sales representatives have their own lists because they already sell products and services in the same industry. List ownership and control may be defined in the sales representative agreement.

List Validating

List validation is the process of contacting or confirming some or all of the information that is contained in a list (such as a sales prospect list) is accurate. List validation may be performed by the sales representative, the company or a combination of both.

List Management

List management is the acquiring, sending and updating of lists of people or companies that share common interests. List management may be performed by the company, by the sales representative or by a combination of both. List management may be performed using contact management programs such as ACT, Goldmine or Salesforce.com.

Contact Management

Contact management is a system that can add, modify and organize lists of people or companies along with activities associated with these contacts. Contact management applications can usually schedule events and keep track of all the communication that occurs between a salesperson and/or customer service representative with people and companies.

Figure 1.5 shows a sample contact management screen. This diagram shows that a contact screen shows contact details along with event related information such as meeting schedules, phone calls, and literature sent.

Figure 1.5, Contact Management

There is a trend towards using online contact management systems, which allow both the sales representative and company to share access to the same contact list.

Sales representatives may use their own contact management system, which may not be directly compatible with the contact management system used by the company. This involves the conversion of contact lists into other formats so they can be transferred to the sales representative.

List Transfer

List transfer is process of selecting, grouping, and moving groups of contacts or data from one system to another. Transferring lists to sales representatives may involve adapting data into a format that the sales representative can use (such as a contact management software program). List transfer may also involve in identifying and gathering of related contact communication records (such as call sheets).

Sales Management

Sales management is the process that records, coordinates and processes information that is used for prospecting, qualifying, interest level assessment, data gathering, and order tracking.

Figure 1.6 shows how a sales process can be tracked and managed. In this example, the sales process is divided into key steps that can be defined and managed. The prospecting step is used to identify new customers or expanded needs for existing customers. The qualification step is used to determine how many of the prospects are qualified (real candidates) for the product or service. The interest assessment step is used to determine how motivated the prospect is to take action to satisfy their need for the product or service. The fact-finding stage is used to determine who are the decision-makers and what steps are necessary to complete the sale. The close involves the consolidation of the previous steps (coordination of motivated decision-makers) so purchases can result. The progress between each step can be tracked and optimized. Included in the chart is an example activity time sheet showing that step may require different levels of time commitment and that the allocation of resources (time for each salesperson) is usually distributed along each step.

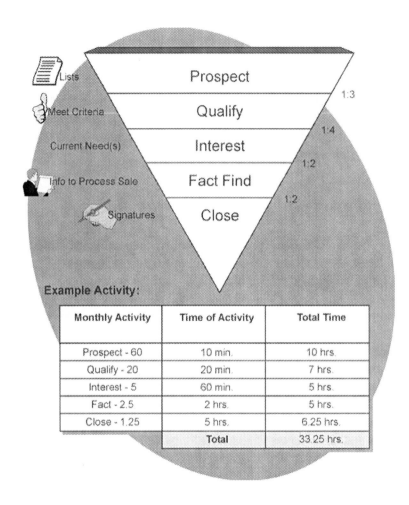

Figure 1.6, Sales Management Diagram

Sales Tracking

Sales tracking is the process of determining the progress of sales related activities. Sales tracking can be used to determine how many prospective customers have been identified and where they are located in the sales cycle.

A key method for tracking sales activity is to require a sales person to complete and submit call sheets. A call sheet is a data gathering form that is used to record information that results from a call or communication session with a person or company. Call sheets may be used during sales contacts to gather and qualify information. Because call sheets require time and effort to complete, sales representatives may be reluctant to complete and submit them.

Figure 1.7 shows a sample call sheet. This example shows that a call sheet that contains company and personal contact information along with other

Figure 1.7, Sales Call Sheet

kinds of qualifying information. Some of the additional qualifying information include type of company (check boxes), purpose of call, call summary, follow-up assignments, and when to follow-up.

Termination Clauses

A termination clause is a condition or set of conditions that may result in the authorization or requirement that the requirements of a contract or agreement may end. There are several reasons why sales representative agreements may be terminated before their normal terms ranging from mutual agreement to violations of the agreement.

An early termination option is a term in an agreement that allows for the termination of some or all of an agreement provided that some condition exists. An early termination option usually defines the amount of time that notice must be given and the responsibilities if the option is taken.

A non-performance clause defines specific objectives in an agreement that must be met and what happens if these objectives are not achieved. A term violation clause may define what happens if one or more of the terms of the agreement are violated such as reductions or forfeiture of commissions. A sales representative agreement may define what would be perceived as a conflict of interest such as selling competing products or represent a competing company.

Sales representative agreements may be terminated for non-payment issues such as if the company has not paid the sales representative. An audit clause may be included to ensure that sales commissions are calculated and paid as agreed.

Other reasons why sales representative agreements may be terminated include intent to defraud such as when a company uses a sales representative to sell products that do not exist (such as vaporware).

Figure 1.8 shows some sample termination clauses. This shows that an early termination option allows one or either party to terminate early if they exercise the option. Non-performance may be used to terminate sales representative agreements provided the targets (sales targets) are not achieved. If some or all of the terms of the agreement are violated, the agreement may be terminated. Agreements may be terminated if the sales representative begins to sell competing products or works for a competing company. Sales representative agreements may also be terminated if the company does not pay sales commission or it does not produce or provide products that the sales representative was contracted to sell.

Termination Clause	Examples
Early Termination Option	One or both parties exercise their option to terminate early
Non-Performance	Did not reach sales targets
Term Violation	One or both of the parties violates a required term
Conflict of Interest	One or both of the parties sell competing products
Non Payment	Company did not pay sales commissions
Intent to Defraud	Retained to sell products that will not exist

Figure 1.8, Sample Sales Agreement Termination Clause

Non-Competition Agreement (Non-Compete)

A non-competition agreement or clause is commitment of a company or person that they will not work or assist other people or companies in a competing business or industry. A non-compete agreement usually restricts competitive actions for a limited period of time (such as 1 to 3 years). Non-compete agreements may be requested by companies to help ensure a sales representative does not develop business relationships with key customers prior to changing companies and working for a competitor. Non-compete agreements may be a separate agreement or a non-compete clause included as a term in the sales rep agreement. States or governments have varying requirements for what is a reasonable length of time that acceptable for non-compete agreements.

Retainer

A retainer is a value that is provided to a person or company in advance of the receiving of products of services. A retainer may be requested or given as a gesture of good faith or to ensure a person or company will be paid for their services. It also "reserves" an agreed upon number of hours or at least a priority of attention provided by the recipient.

A retainer fee may be used or applied towards future sales commissions (refundable) or it may be an amount that is guaranteed to be paid (non-refundable). A rollover retainer is value that is transferred to the following period of time if the retainer is not used in full.

Draw

A draw is a value that is provided to a person or company that is paid in advance of scheduled payments. Draws against commissions may have limits on how much can be taken and when it has to be repaid. Some draw allowances may require a hard repayment dates which forces a draw balance back to 0 at least 1 time per year.

Sales Representative Support

Sales representative support is the resources that will be provided to the sales representative or to others designated by the sales representative. Sales representative support may include product literature, technical support, customer service, engineering support, and other types of services.

Sales Literature

Sales literature is a media item (such as a pamphlet) that is used by a sales person to help communicate or motivate a prospective customer to buy a product or service. Sales literature may include product brochures, catalogs, application notes, and specification sheets. Sales literature can also be in electric formats such as web pages, spec sheets or application notes.

Sales literature may be provided directly to the sales representative for distribution or it may be provided to prospective customers via an administrative person at the company office who packages and sends it directly to the customer. The company may keep on file standard greeting letters from the sales representatives that are packaged with the sales literature.

Product Samples

A product sample is an item or service that is provided to a customer or prospective customer for free or at reduced cost to help them decide or evaluate the purchase of additional products or services.

To obtain or send product samples, a sales representative may have to complete a product request along with providing a reason and/or obtaining an authorization. The number, type and value of product samples a sales representative can send may have limits that are based on the value or qualifications of the company.

Business Cards

Business cards are small amounts of media that contain company and contact information. Business cards may in the form of standard size printed cards or they may also be in various electronic formats.

Sales representative business cards may be provided by the company they represent or the sales representative may use their own card. Sales representatives commonly use their own business cards when the represent multiple companies in the same industry. When this occurs, the sales representative may include the company name or logo of the companies they represent on their business card.

If the company provides business cards to the sales representative, the address on the card may be the address of the corporation and the company may forward mail it receives to the sales representative.

Email Address

An email address is the combination of a text or numeric identifier with a web address that can be used to route messages to a person or device. Sales representatives may be given a company email address or they may use their own email address. When assigned a company email address, the company may setup the email address to automatically forward all emails to their existing email address. Using email forwarding, a company can redirect the email address after the person leaves the company to ensure communication with customers or prospective customers is not lost.

Sales Leads

A sales lead is contact information about a potential customer. Sales leads may be qualified (some validated information or interest) or they may be unqualified (no validated). Companies may regularly receive sales leads as a result of normal business operations (web site) or through marketing efforts (such as press releases). How sales leads will be processed and whom they will be provided to may be defined in the sales representative agreement.

Technical Support

Technical support is the communication, system and processes that are used to help customers or users of products to use, configure or solve problems related to the product they purchased. Sales representatives may be provided with contact information for people at the company and possibly consultants who can answer technical support questions.

Training

Training is the providing of information materials in a format that helps a person to gain knowledge or skills. Training may be provided in various forms including instructor led training, online training, web seminars, and self-study courses.

Sales Training

Sales training is the providing or presentation of information that help sales people to understand the benefits and operation of products or services. Some companies may require sales training to ensure the sales representative knows the operation and features of the products or services they are selling. Companies may pay for sales training time (possibly at a reduced rate) and travel expenses while other companies require the sales representative do not get paid for training time and to pay their own travel expenses.

Product Trainers

Product trainers are people who provide information and educational support to users or sellers of products or services. Product trainers may be used to help users or retailers to become more familiar with the capabilities and features of a product or service. This makes them more likely to sell or use the product.

Product trainers may be part of sales or marketing departments. Sales representatives may request that product training services to be provided to retailers or corporate clients. Retailers may allow the product trainers to work with their salespeople because it can increase the retailer's sales effectiveness.

Administrative Services

Administrative services are the supporting clerical and other management duties that are necessary to perform business tasks or processes. Sales representatives may be provided with access to administrative personnel at the company who can send out product literature and samples and perform data processing functions such as data mining or filtering lists.

Figure 1.9 shows a list of support services that may be available or provided to the sales representative. This list shows sales support could include sales training, sales support, product trainers and administrative support.

Support Service	Descripotion
Sales Training	Product and technology awareness
Sales Support	Technical solutions
Product or User Trainers	Retailer and customer training
Administration	Office and IT support

Figure 1.9, Sales Representative Support Services

Approved Customer List

An approved customer is a person or company that has been authorized to buy products or services from a company. Sales representatives may only be allowed to sell to companies on an approved customer list. The approved customer list may be attached to an appendix of the sales representative agreement or it may be a separate document that is continually updated.

Exclusions

Exclusions are conditions or requirements that inhibit, restrict or alter the terms of an agreement, offer, or operation. Sales representative agreement exclusions may include companies that a sales representative may not be allowed to do business with. These could be competitors, companies involved in certain types of content (such as weapons or pornography) or other characteristics such as company size (such as not too big or not too small).

Additional Sales Representative Agreement Terms

Additional terms that may be included in sales representative agreements include governing laws, written consent, confidentiality, arbitration, and formal communication requirements (notices).

Governing Laws

Governing laws are governmental rules (identified by city, state or country) and regulations that are used to enforce the terms of an agreement. Agreements commonly specify which government entity or jurisdiction shall apply to the agreement and other laws/requirements that may apply. Companies commonly desire to have the governing laws apply in the country and/or state that they are located in.

Written Consent

Written consent is the providing of authorization in marking (e.g. signature) or document form. Agreements may contain a written consent clause to require changes to be made in writing to avoid ambiguity.

Confidentiality

Confidentiality is the protection or processing of data to ensure that an unauthorized user or receiver cannot use the information. Confidentiality may be required to protect customer lists, product information and business agreements. To protect confidentiality, sales representatives may be asked to sign a non-disclosure agreement.

Non-Disclosure Agreement (NDA)

A non-disclosure agreement is a binding contract between parties not to disclose and to keep confidential information shared among the parties from being spread to other parties. Commonly referred to as an NDA, in certain circumstances such an agreement can preserve the novelty of an invention. Documents exchanged under a properly written and executed NDA may not be considered as a publication or public dissemination of an invention and can preserve the right of the inventor to apply for patent protection.

Arbitration

Arbitration is a process or a set of rules that is used to manage conflicts where a designated third party can mediate disputes between people or companies. An arbitration clause in a sales representative agreement defines how and where conflicts may be resolved through the use of arbitration. Arbitration can be a less complex, faster and lower cost method for resolving conflicts than the legal system.

Notices

Notices are declarations or messages that are provided or sent to people or companies to alert them of events or conditions. Notices may be required for certain business or legal transactions. For sales representative agreements, a method of notice may define the contact information of the person or company that should be notified in the event there are changes in the terms or conditions of the agreement.

Option to Renew

An option to renew is a term or condition that authorizes a person or company to renew an agreement or portions of an agreement when certain conditions exist. A renewal option may be included in a sales representative agreement along with certain criteria such as meeting specific sales objectives.

Order Processing

Order processing are the steps involved in selecting the products and agreeing to the terms that are required for a person or company to obtain products or services. Order processing steps may include submission, order approval, credit approval, order confirmation, and order fulfillment.

Order Submission

Order submission is the process of transferring of the details that authorize an order to be processed. Order submission methods can range from a verbal order to detailed orders that are transferred via electronic data interchange (EDI) systems.

Orders should indicate who is responsible for the order (such as the sales rep). This allows the company to track sales that are generated by a sales rep and pay commissions on those sales (if necessary).

Order Approval

Order approval is an authorization to accept the terms of an offer to purchase goods or services. Orders may be sent to a company manager for review and approval. If a submitted order is disapproved (such as for the price), the sales representative may renegotiate the terms of the sale and resubmit the order.

Credit Approval

Credit approval is an authorization to provide payment terms to a person or company so they can purchase goods or services. Some orders may be contingent on obtaining credit terms for the purchase of the products or services. Payment options may include prepay, cash on delivery (COD), due upon receipt, 2% discount if paid in 10 days and full balance due within 30 days (2/10 net 30), and possibly other extended payment options that may include interest and other fees (such as additional fees for late payments).

Order Confirmation

Order confirmation is a notice or message that confirms an order has been received and processed. Order confirmation may be sent to the customer and/or sales representative who processed the order. An order confirmation may include a projected fulfillment and ship date.

Order Fulfillment

Order fulfillment is the process of gathering the products and materials to complete an order and shipping the products or initiating the services that were ordered. A sales representative may want to receive shipping tracking numbers so they can monitor the shipping and fulfillment status.

Order Status

Order status is the condition of the progress of an order through is processing cycle. Order states may include received, accepted, processed, and fulfilled. Sales representatives may check the status of orders by calling in to the order processing department or by having remote access to order processing systems (such as web portals).

Appendix 1 - Manufacturer Rep Agreement

\<Company\>
Manufacturer's Representative Agreement

This instrument, hereafter referred to as the "AGREEMENT", executed this \<Agreement Date\>, between **\<Company\>**, located at _____ _____, (hereafter referred to as \<Company\>) and _____, located at **\<Representative Address\>** (hereafter referred to as REPRESENTATIVE). It is the intention of both parties of this Manufacturer's Representative Agreement to promote the sale of \<Company\> products (hereafter referred to as "PRODUCTS").

   \<Company\> hereby appoints REPRESENTATIVE as its independent representative to solicit orders and otherwise assist in obtaining orders for products sold, licensed or otherwise distributed by \<Company\>, for the accounts as set forth in Addendum A here to, and accepts such appointment and agrees to solicit orders and promote the PRODUCTS in accordance with the terms of this AGREEMENT.

   REPRESENTATIVE agrees to promote the sale of \<Company\> products in accordance with the instructional materials provided to REPRESENTATIVE by \<Company\>.

   REPRESENTATIVE shall submit to \<Company\> periodic reports relating to its activities directed to introduce, sell and support PRODUCTS.

   \<Company\> agrees to make available to REPRESENTATIVE sufficient samples of products, brochures, price lists and promotional aids. All aforementioned materials shall be used for the express purpose of promoting sales of PRODUCT, never intended for individual re-sale. \<Company\> shall have the right to limit the number of samples furnished, when determined by <Company> that such samples are not necessary for REPRESENTATIVE to effectively promote the PRODUCT.

REPRESENTATIVE agrees to indemnify <Company> against losses from claims arising from infringement as may be made, should REPRESENTATIVE attempt to sell or market PRODUCT beyond the agreed upon account list or territory ascribed.

REPRESENTATIVE agrees to use only professional conduct in selling PRODUCTS, within the general guidelines provided by <Company> defining the nature and image of the PRODUCTS and trademarks. Under no circumstances shall REPRESENTATIVE act in any official capacity as a direct agent for <Company>.

<Company> agrees to pay commissions on the gross sales less freight to customer for product orders delivered and paid by customers, which qualify under the terms and conditions of this AGREEMENT. Commission is earned only when the transaction is complete, i.e. the goods have been shipped and paid for, regardless of the time of payment. Earned commissions shall be paid on the 15th day following receipt of payment by <Company>.

The terms of this AGREEMENT shall commence on the Effective Date and shall continue for <Term>. This agreement is not automatically renewed or extended without signed authorization by <Company>.

This AGREEMENT may be terminated by either party, at any time, with or without cause, and without liability to the other party, upon ninety (90) days written notice to the other party.

Upon termination of this AGREEMENT, as a further condition of payment of any commissions then due, REPRESENTATIVE shall, at its own expense, immediately return to <Company> all materials and samples relating to the PRODUCTS, including but not limited to <Company> products, literature, catalogs, price lists, graphics or collateral materials provided by <Company> or prepared by REPRESENTATIVE in connection with this AGREEMENT.

REPRESENTATIVE shall be entitled to full commissions on gross sales less freight to customer of PRODUCTS to customers pursuant to purchase orders received and accepted by <Company> prior to effective date of termination of this

AGREEMENT, providing orders are scheduled to ship within 90 days of termination date.

<Company> and REPRESENTATIVE agree that all travel and any other necessary expenses that REPRESENTATIVE must incur in order to sell, promote and place <Company> PRODUCTS, are the sole expense of REPRESENTATIVE.

This AGREEMENT, its interpretation, construction and effort shall be governed by and under the laws <Governing Location>.

The effective date of this AGREEMENT shall be the date on which it is signed by <Company>.

This agreement shall inure to the benefit of and be binding upon the successor in business of both <Company> and the assignees of <Company>, but shall not otherwise be assignable by REPRESENTATIVE without prior written consent from <Company>.

This writing constitutes the entire AGREEMENT between the parties hereto relating to the subject matter of the AGREEMENT and no term of provision of this AGREEMENT shall be varied or modified by any prior or subsequent statement. The parties herein may amend this AGREEMENT by written instrument specifically referred to this AGREEMENT and signed by <Company>.

Accepted by: Accepted by:

_____
_____
<Company Employee>   <Representative>
<Company>

Date: _____   Date: _____

<Company>
Manufacturer's Representative Agreement

Addendum A

Name(s) of target account(s) ascribed to REPRESENTATIVE (**<Representative>**):

    <Company Sample>

    Other accounts by mutual agreement (in writing)

Commission Schedule:
    <Commission> % on all gross sales less freight to customer or agreed upon percentage on a
    case by case basis

Accepted by: Accepted by:

_____
_____
<Company Employee>   <Representative>
<Company>

Date: _____   Date: _____

Appendix 2 - Sales Rep Agreement

SALES REPRESENTATIVE AGREEMENT

This AGREEMENT made this <Agreement Date> by and between **<Company>** a corporation incorporated under the laws of <Territory>, and having its principal office located at manufacturer <Company Address>, and <Representative>, <Representative Address> ("Representative") as follows:

A)   APPOINTMENT AND ACCEPTANCE - manufacturer appoints Representative as its "representative" to promote the sale of and sell its products (indicated in Provision #3 hereof); in the territory (indicated in Provision #2 hereof); and Representative accepts the appointment and agrees to sell and promote the sale of the manufacturer's products.

B)   TERRITORY - Representative's Territory shall consist exclusively of the following:

<Territory>

PRODUCTS

The "products" of the manufacturer to be promoted for sale and sold by the Representative are:
Entire <Company> product line

EXCLUSIONS:

None

AMOUNT OF COMPENSATION

Representative's compensation for services performed hereunder shall be <commission> % of the "net invoice price" of the manufacturer's products shipped into Representative's territory.

COMPUTATION AND PAYMENT OF COMMISSION

Commissions are due and payable on or before the 15th day of the month immediately following the month in which customer is invoiced. Manufacturer will send Representative copies of invoices respective to the Representative's territory at the time manufacturer invoices customer.

At the time of payment of commissions to Representative, manufacturer will send Representative a commission statement showing:

Commissions due and owing Representative for that period and any prior periods, and commissions being paid (listing the invoices on which commissions are being paid).
"Net invoice price" shall mean the total price at which an order is invoiced to the customer, but excluding shipping and insurance costs, sales tax, use and excise taxes, any allowances or discounts granted to the customer by the manufacturer, and any tariffs, duties and export fees involved in international shipments.
There shall be deducted from any sums due Representative:
An amount equal to commissions previously paid or credited on sales of manufacturer's products which have since been returned by the customer or on allowances credited to the customer for any reason by the manufacturer; and;
An amount equivalent to commissions previously paid or credited on sales which manufacturer shall not have been fully paid by the customer whether by reason of the customer's bankruptcy, insolvency,

or any other reason which, in manufacturer judgment renders the account past due or uncollectible. If any sums are ever realized upon such uncollectible accounts, manufacturer will pay Representative its percentage of commission applicable at the time of the original sale upon the net proceeds of such collection.

"Order" shall mean any commitment to purchase manufacturer's products which calls for shipment into Representative's territory or which is subject to a split commission in accordance with Provision #4 hereof.

ACCEPTANCE OF ORDERS

All orders are subject to acceptance or rejection by an authorized officer of manufacturer and to the approval of manufacturer's credit department. Manufacturer shall be responsible for all credit risks and collections.

If manufacturer notifies customer of its acceptance or rejection of an order, a copy of any written notification shall be transmitted to the Representative. At least once every month manufacturer shall supply Representative with copies of all orders received directly by manufacturer, copies of all shipping notices, and copies of all quotations made to customers in the territory.

TERMS OF SALE

All sales shall be at prices and upon terms established by the manufacturer, and it shall have the right, in its discretion, from time to time, to establish, change, alter or amend prices and other terms and conditions of sale. Representative shall not accept orders in the manufacturer's name or make price quotations or delivery promises without the manufacturer's prior approval.

REPRESENTATIVES RELATIONSHIP AND CONDUCT OF BUSI-

NESS

Representative shall maintain a sales office in the territory and devote such time as may be reasonably necessary to sell and promote manufacturer's products within the territory.

Representative will: conduct all of its business in its own name and in such manner it may see fit, pay all expenses whatever of its office and activities, and be responsible for the acts and expenses of its employees and sub-representatives.

Nothing in this Agreement shall be construed to constitute Representative as the partner, employee or agent of the manufacturer nor shall either party have any authority to bind the other in any respect, it being intended that each shall remain an independent contractor responsible only for its own actions.

Representative shall not, without manufacturer's prior written approval, alter, enlarge, or limit orders, make representations or guarantees concerning manufacturer's products or accept the return of, or make any allowance for such products.

Representative shall furnish to manufacturer's Credit Department any information that it may have from time to time relative to the credit standing of any of its customers.

Representative shall abide by manufacturer's policies and communicate same to manufacturer's customers.

Manufacturer shall be solely responsible for the design, development, supply, production and performance of its products and the protection of its patents, trademarks and trade names.

Manufacturer agrees to indemnify and hold Representative harmless from and against and to pay all losses, costs, damages or expenses whatsoever, including reasonable attorney's fees, which Representative may sustain or incur on account of infringement or alleged infringement of patents trademarks, or trade names, or breach of warranty in any way resulting from the sale of manufacturer's products. Manufacturer will also indemnify Representative from and hold it harmless from and against all liabilities, losses, damages, costs or expenses, including reasonable attorney's fees, which it may at any time suffer, incur, or be required to pay by reason of injury or death to any person or damage to property or both caused or allegedly caused by any products sold by manufacturer. Manufacturer shall furnish Representative, at no expense to Representative, samples, catalogs, literature and any other material necessary for the proper promotion and sale of its products in the territory. Any literature that is not used or samples or other equipment belonging to manufacturer shall be returned to the manufacturer at its request.

If for any reason Representative, at manufacturer's request, takes possession of manufacturer's products, the risk of loss or damage to or destruction of such products shall be borne by manufacturer, and manufacturer shall indemnify and hold Representative harmless against any claims, debts, liabilities or causes of action resulting from any such loss, damage, or destruction.

Manufacturer will keep Representative fully informed about sales and promotional policies and programs affecting the Representative's territory.

TERM OF AGREEMENT AND TERMINATION

This Agreement shall be effective on <effective date>, and shall continue in force for <term> period, and shall be automatically renewed for additional one (1) year periods thereafter unless terminated by written notice from either party to the other not less than thirty (30) days prior to the end of the initial or any subsequent one year term. This Agreement may also be terminated:

By manufacturer immediately upon written notice to Representative by registered or certified mail if there is a change of fifty (50%) percent or more of the present ownership or control of the Representative's business without manufacturer's written consent.

By manufacturer if Representative, without manufacturer's written consent, offers, promotes or sells any product which is competitive with any product Representative is to offer, promote or sell for manufacturer in accordance with the breach is not cured within ten (10) days after receipt of such notice by Representative, and written notice of termination is mailed to or served upon Representative.

By Representative:

If manufacturer, without Representative's written consent offers, promotes or sells any product which is competitive with any product Representative is offering or selling for any other manufacturer, and written notice of this breach of the Agreement is mailed to or served upon manufacturer, the breach is not cured within ten (10) days after receipt of such notice by the manufacturer, and written notice of termination is mailed to or served upon manufacturer, or immediately upon written notice to manufacturer by Registered or Certified mail in the event manufacturer sells substantially all of the assets of its business or there is a change of 50% or more of its present ownership or it is merged with another firm, corporation or business and manufacturer is not the surviving company.

By either party:

In the event of the other party's unreasonable and repeated failure to perform the terms and conditions of this Agreement, written notice of the failure is mailed to or served upon that party, the failure is not cured within thirty (30) days after receipt of such notice, and written notice of termination is mailed to or served on that party, or upon immediate written notice to the other party in the event that party has filed or has filed against it a petition in bankruptcy (which is not dismissed within thirty (30) days after it is filed) or that party makes an assignment for the benefit of creditors; or By mutual written agreement.

RIGHTS UPON TERMINATION

Upon termination of this Agreement for any reason, Representative shall be entitled to:
Commissions on shipments into Representative's territory that is dated prior to the effective date of termination.

Commissions referred to in this Provision #11 shall be paid on or before the fifteenth (15th) day of the month following the month in which the manufacturer receives payment for the orders.

GENERAL

This Agreement contains the entire understanding of the parties, shall supersede any other oral or written agreements, and shall be binding upon and inure to the benefit of the parties successors and assigns. It may not be modified in any way without the written consent of both parties. Representative shall not have the right to assign this Agreement in whole or in part without manufacturer's written consent.

CONSTRUCTION OF AGREEMENT

This Agreement shall be construed according to the laws of <governing location>.

DISPUTES AND ARBITRATION

The parties agree that any disputes or questions arising hereunder including the construction or application of this Agreement shall be settled by arbitration in accordance with the rules of the American Arbitration Association then in force, and that the arbitration hearings shall be held in the city in which the principal office of the party requesting arbitration (with the American Arbitration Association) is located. If the parties cannot agree upon an arbitrator within ten (10) days after demand by either of them, either or both parties may request the American Arbitration Association to name a panel of five (5) arbitrators. The manufacturer shall strike the names of two (2) on this list, the Representative shall then strike two (2) names, and the remaining name shall be the arbitrator. The decision of the arbitrator shall be final and binding upon the parties both as to law and to fact, and shall not be appealable to any court in any jurisdiction. The expenses of the arbitrator shall be shared equally by the parties, unless the arbitrator determines that the expenses shall be otherwise assessed.

NOTICES

All notices, demands or other communications by either party to the other shall be in writing and shall be effective upon personal delivery or if sent by mail seventy-two (72) hours after deposited in the United States mail, first class postage, prepaid, Registered or Certified, and all such notices given by mail shall be sent and addressed as follows until such time as another address is given by notice pursuant to this provision 15:

To manufacturer: To Representative:

<Company Address>   <Representative Address>

IN WITNESS WHEREOF, The parties hereto have executed this Agreement on the day and year first above written in multiple counterparts, each of which shall be considered an original.

Manufacturer:

By: __   _____

Title: _____

Signed:

REPRESENTATIVE:_____

By: _____

Title:

Signed:

Appendix 3 - Marketing Services Agreement

MARKETING SERVICES AGREEMENT

This Agreement is entered into by and between <Company> Development, and its affiliates, subsidiaries, successors, and assignees (collectively "<COMPANY>") and <Representative> on behalf of a to-be-formed-entity ("Consultant").

In full and complete consideration of the mutual promises set forth herein below, the parties agree as follows:

1. SERVICES. <COMPANY> engages Consultant on an exclusive basis (only to Approved Companies as defined below) to secure a licensing and/or royalty agreement(s) between <COMPANY> and certain approved companies, their affiliates, subsidiaries, successors and assignees (collectively "Approved Company or Approved Companies" listed on Appendix B attached hereto as may be updated from time to time by mutual agreement. In addition, <COMPANY> engages Consultant on an exclusive basis (only on Approved Products to Approved Companies) to arrange direct sales agreements between <COMPANY> and certain Approved Companies, their affiliates, subsidiaries, successors and assignees on specific product(s) listed on Appendix B attached hereto as may be updated from time to time by mutual agreement (hereinafter referred to as "Approved Product(s)"). Agreements between <COMPANY> and Approved Companies pertaining to either license or royalty agreements or Approved Products shall hereinafter be referred to as "Approved Agreement(s)".

2.   TERM. The term (the "Term") of this Agreement shall continue on the day following the full execution of this Agreement to 11:59 p.m. Central Time one year later. In the event an Approved Agreement is signed within the Term or within one hundred eighty (180) days of the termination of this Agreement, the Term of this Agreement, as it pertains only to a specific Approved Agreement, will run concurrent with the term of the Approved Agreement and one renewal thereof. Further extensions will be based upon mutual written agreement between the parties to this Agreement.

3.   COMPENSATION. During each calendar year, Consultant shall receive Commissions (Royalty or Sales), pursuant to Exhibit A, from <COMPANY> on royalties, licensing fees and direct sales (as described in the Approved Agreements) received by <COMPANY> from each Approved Company or on each Approved Product. Commissions owed to Consultant shall be paid within thirty (30) days after the last day of each calendar month in which <COMPANY> receives a payment from the Approved Company. Commissions shall be payable only with respect to the Approved Agreements. Consultant shall have the right to audit <COMPANY> pursuant to the Approved Agreements at Consultant's expense except that if the audit shows that the Commissions were not paid in accordance with Exhibit A (+/- 5% deviation), <COMPANY> shall pay the cost of the audit.

4.   EXPENSES. In the event that Consultant is required, in connection with its performance hereunder, to incur business expenses, e.g. travel and lodging, <COMPANY> shall reimburse Consultant for all reasonable and necessary expenses that have been approved in writing, in advance, by <COMPA-

NY>. In connection with such expenses, Consultant shall submit to <COMPANY> documentation substantiating same, *e.g.*, receipts. Provided, however, that all expenses reimbursed by <COMPANY> shall be deducted from Commissions otherwise payable to Consultant.

5. <u>CONFIDENTIALITY</u>. Consultant acknowledges and agrees that during the course of the provision of Consultant's services, Consultant may be exposed to sensitive data and information concerning the business and affairs of <COMPANY>, (the Proprietary Information) and that all of such data and information are vital, sensitive, confidential and proprietary to <COMPANY>. Consultant expressly acknowledges the trade secret status of the Proprietary Information and acknowledges that the Proprietary Information constitutes a protectable business interest of <COMPANY>, and covenants and agrees that during the term of the engagement hereunder and for the ten years after the expiration or termination of such engagement or the consultants last payment receipt (which ever is later), Consultant shall not, directly or indirectly, whether, in the case of Consultant, individually, as a director, stockholder, owner, partner, employee, principal or agent of or consultant to any business, or in any other capacity, make known, disclose, furnish, make available or utilize any of the Proprietary Information, other than in the proper performance of the duties contemplated herein during the term of the engagement hereunder. Consultant's obligations hereunder with respect to particular Proprietary Information shall terminate only at such time (if any) as the Proprietary Information in question becomes generally known to the public other than through a breach of Consultant's obligations hereunder. Consultant acknowledges and agrees that all records or documents containing Proprietary Information prepared by Consultant or coming into his possession by virtue of the engagement are and shall remain the property of <COMPA-

NY> and that, upon termination or expiration of this engagement, Consultant shall return immediately to <COMPANY> all such items in its possession, together with all copies and extracts, and will destroy all summaries thereof and any such information stored electronically on tapes, computer disks or in any other manner.

6.   INDEPENDENT CONTRACTOR. In performing the Services under this Agreement, Consultant will be acting as an independent contractor and not as an employee of <COMPANY> for any purpose whatsoever, including but not limited to workers compensation, health insurance and other benefits offered by <COMPANY> to its employees and the withholding and payment of income taxes with respect to the compensation being paid to Consultant hereunder. Further, Consultant will not have any authority or ability to bind, contract on behalf of or otherwise obligate <COMPANY> in any manner.

7.   ENTIRE AGREEMENT. This Agreement contains the entire and complete understanding of the parties and may not be amended except by a writing signed by both parties.

8.   GOVERNING LAW. This Agreement is intended to be interpreted and construed in accordance with the laws of the State of Texas applicable to agreements wholly made and to be performed therein.

IN WITNESS WHEREOF, the parties have executed this Agreement effective as of the latest date indicated below.

_____   _____

<COMPANY>   <Representative>
Title:
Title:
Date:
Date:

EXHIBIT A

Schedule of Commissions

Consultant shall be paid a commission ("Commissions") on royalties and licensing fees received by <COMPANY> pursuant to each Approved Agreement pertaining to royalties and licensing fees as follows:

1. Consultant shall be paid <Commission> % of the gross amount of royalties received by <COMPANY> from an Approved Company to this Agreement during a calendar year. In the event royalties and licensing fees exceed $1,000,000.00 during a calendar year, bonus commissions shall be paid as follows:

Incremental Volume over $1,000,000Additional Percent Bonus$1,000,001 – $1,999,999Three Percent (1%)$2,000,000 - $2,999,999Two Percent (2%)$3,000,000 and overOne Percent (3%)

The following examples are intended to illustrate the calculation of commissions payable pursuant to this Agreement:

Example One: In calendar year two, royalties equal $1,000,000.00. The commission payable to Consultant is 5% x $1,000,000.00 = $50,000.

Example Two: In calendar year three, royalties equal $8,000,000. The commission payable to Consultant is 5% x $8,000,000 ($400,000) plus 1% x $1,000,000 ($10,000) for the volume between $1,000,000 and $1,999,999 plus 2% x $1,000,000 ($20,000) for the volume between $2,000,000 and $2,999,999 plus 3% x $5,000,000 ($150,000) for the volume between $3,000,000 and $8,000,000. Total

> commissions payable to Consultant in calendar year
> three are $580,000 ($400,000 plus $10,000 plus
> $20,000 plus $150,000)

2. Any royalty payments received in advance by <COMPANY> will, for purposes of calculating the Royalty Commissions owed to Consultant under this Agreement, be deemed to have been received as earned, in accordance with generally accepted accounting principles.

Licensing Fees:

> 1. Consultant shall be paid <Commission> (6%) of any licensing fees paid to <COMPANY> with respect to any Approved Agreement(s) that are fully executed between <COMPANY> and a Company introduced by Consultant. Licensing fees shall not include any advance royalty payments.

Direct Sales:

Consultant shall be paid a commission, on receipt of payment by <COMPANY> from an Approved Company, ("Sales Commission") during the Term on direct sales received by <COMPANY> from any Approved Company on Approved Product(s) pursuant to each Approved Agreement as follows:

> > Consultant shall be paid <Commission> % of the net sales price on direct sales received by <COMPANY> from an Approved Company to this Agreement during a calendar year. Net sales is hereby defined as the actual sales price <COMPANY> (or its affiliates) invoices to its customers, but less the cost of (a) taxes; (b) export duties; (c) other governmental charges separately imposed on <COMPANY> with respect to its products; (d) credits on returns; (e) shipping expense; and (f) insurance on shipping.

APPENDIX B

Approved Companies

ABC Manufacturing
DEF Supply
GHI Enterprises
JKL International
MNO United

Index

Althos Publishing Book List

Product ID	Title	# Pages	ISBN	Price	Copyright
Billing					
BK7781338	Billing Dictionary	644	1932813381	$39.99	2006
BK7781339	Creating RFPs for Billing Systems	94	193281339X	$19.99	2007
BK7781373	Introduction to IPTV Billing	60	193281373X	$14.99	2006
BK7781384	Introduction to Telecom Billing, 2nd Edition	68	1932813845	$19.99	2007
BK7781343	Introduction to Utility Billing	92	1932813438	$19.99	2007
BK7769438	Introduction to Wireless Billing	44	097469438X	$14.99	2004
IP Telephony					
BK7781311	Creating RFPs for IP Telephony Communication Systems	86	193281311X	$19.99	2004
BK7780530	Internet Telephone Basics	224	0972805303	$29.99	2003
BK7727877	Introduction to IP Telephony, 2nd Edition	112	0974278777	$19.99	2006
BK7780538	Introduction to SIP IP Telephony Systems	144	0972805389	$14.99	2003
BK7769430	Introduction to SS7 and IP	56	0974694304	$12.99	2004
BK7781309	IP Telephony Basics	324	1932813098	$34.99	2004
BK7781361	Tehrani's IP Telephony Dictionary, 2nd Edition	628	1932813616	$39.99	2005
BK7780532	Voice over Data Networks for Managers	348	097280532X	$49.99	2003
IP Television					
BK7781362	Creating RFPs for IP Television Systems	86	1932813624	$19.99	2007
BK7781355	Introduction to Data Multicasting	68	1932813551	$19.99	2006
BK7781340	Introduction to Digital Rights Management (DRM)	84	1932813403	$19.99	2006
BK7781351	Introduction to IP Audio	64	1932813519	$19.99	2006
BK7781335	Introduction to IP Television	104	1932813357	$19.99	2006
BK7781341	Introduction to IP Video	88	1932813411	$19.99	2006
BK7781352	Introduction to Mobile Video	68	1932813527	$19.99	2006
BK7781353	Introduction to MPEG	72	1932813535	$19.99	2006
BK7781342	Introduction to Premises Distribution Networks (PDN)	68	193281342X	$19.99	2006
BK7781357	IP Television Directory	154	1932813578	$89.99	2007
BK7781356	IPTV Basics	308	193281356X	$39.99	2006
BK7781389	IPTV Business Opportunities	232	1932813896	$24.99	2007
BK7781334	IPTV Dictionary	652	1932813349	$39.99	2006
Legal and Regulatory					
BK7781378	Not so Patently Obvious	224	1932813780	$39.99	2006
BK7780533	Patent or Perish	220	0972805338	$39.95	2003
BK7769433	Practical Patent Strategies Used by Successful Companies	48	0974694339	$14.99	2003
BK7781332	Strategic Patent Planning for Software Companies	58	1932813322	$14.99	2004
Telecom					
BK7781313	ATM Basics	156	1932813136	$29.99	2004
BK7781345	Introduction to Digital Subscriber Line (DSL)	72	1932813454	$14.99	2005
BK7727872	Introduction to Private Telephone Systems 2nd Edition	86	0974278726	$14.99	2005
BK7727876	Introduction to Public Switched Telephone 2nd Edition	54	0974278769	$14.99	2005
BK7781302	Introduction to SS7	138	1932813020	$19.99	2004
BK7781315	Introduction to Switching Systems	92	1932813152	$19.99	2007
BK7781314	Introduction to Telecom Signaling	88	1932813144	$19.99	2007
BK7727870	Introduction to Transmission Systems	52	097427870X	$14.99	2004
BK7780537	SS7 Basics, 3rd Edition	276	0972805370	$34.99	2003
BK7780535	Telecom Basics, 3rd Edition	354	0972805354	$29.99	2003
BK7781316	Telecom Dictionary	744	1932813160	$39.99	2006
BK7780539	Telecom Systems	384	0972805397	$39.99	2006

Product ID	Title	# Pages	ISBN	Price	Copyright
Wireless					
BK7769434	Introduction to 802.11 Wireless LAN (WLAN)	62	0974694347	$14.99	2004
BK7781374	Introduction to 802.16 WiMax	116	1932813748	$19.99	2006
BK7781307	Introduction to Analog Cellular	84	1932813071	$19.99	2006
BK7769435	Introduction to Bluetooth	60	0974694355	$14.99	2004
BK7781305	Introduction to Code Division Multiple Access (CDMA)	100	1932813055	$14.99	2004
BK7781308	Introduction to EVDO	84	193281308X	$14.99	2004
BK7781306	Introduction to GPRS and EDGE	98	1932813063	$14.99	2004
BK7781370	Introduction to Global Positioning System (GPS)	92	1932813705	$19.99	2007
BK7781304	Introduction to GSM	110	1932813047	$14.99	2004
BK7781391	Introduction to HSPDA	88	1932813918	$19.99	2007
BK7781390	Introduction to IP Multimedia Subsystem (IMS)	116	193281390X	$19.99	2006
BK7769439	Introduction to Mobile Data	62	0974694398	$14.99	2005
BK7769432	Introduction to Mobile Telephone Systems	48	0974694320	$10.99	2003
BK7769437	Introduction to Paging Systems	42	0974694371	$14.99	2004
BK7769436	Introduction to Private Land Mobile Radio	52	0974694363	$14.99	2004
BK7727878	Introduction to Satellite Systems	72	0974278785	$14.99	2005
BK7781312	Introduction to WCDMA	112	1932813128	$14.99	2004
BK7727879	Introduction to Wireless Systems, 2nd Edition	76	0974278793	$19.99	2006
BK7781337	Mobile Systems	468	1932813373	$39.99	2007
BK7769431	Wireless Dictionary	670	0974694312	$39.99	2005
BK7780534	Wireless Systems	536	0972805346	$34.99	2004
BK7781303	Wireless Technology Basics	50	1932813039	$12.99	2004
Optical					
BK7781386	Fiber Optic Basics	316	1932813861	$34.99	2006
BK7781329	Introduction to Optical Communication	132	1932813292	$14.99	2006
BK7781365	Optical Dictionary	712	1932813659	$39.99	2007
Marketing					
BK7781318	Introduction to eMail Marketing	88	1932813187	$19.99	2007
BK7781322	Introduction to Internet AdWord Marketing	92	1932813225	$19.99	2007
BK7781320	Introduction to Internet Affiliate Marketing	88	1932813209	$19.99	2007
BK7781317	Introduction to Internet Marketing	104	1932813292	$19.99	2006
BK7781317	Introduction to Search Engine Optimization (SEO)	84	1932813179	$19.99	2007
BK7781323	Web Marketing Dictionary	688	1932813233	$39.99	2007
Programming					
BK7781300	Introduction to xHTML:	58	1932813004	$14.99	2004
BK7727875	Wireless Markup Language (WML)	287	0974278750	$34.99	2003
Datacom					
BK7781331	Datacom Basics	324	1932813314	$39.99	2007
BK7781355	Introduction to Data Multicasting	104	1932813551	$19.99	
BK7727873	Introduction to Data Networks, 2nd Edition	64	0974278734	$19.99	2006
Cable Television					
BK7780536	Introduction to Cable Television, 2nd Edition	96	0972805362	$19.99	2006
BK7781380	Introduction to DOCSIS	104	1932813802	$19.99	2007
BK7781371	Cable Television Dictionary	628	1932813713	$39.99	2007
Business					
BK7781368	Career Coach	92	1932813683	$14.99	2006
BK7781359	How to Get Private Business Loans	56	1932813594	$14.99	2005
BK7781369	Sales Representative Agreements	96	1932813691	$19.99	2007
BK7781364	Efficient Selling	156	1932813640	$24.99	2007

Order Form

Phone: 1 919-557-2260

Fax: 1 919-557-2261   **Date:**_____

404 Wake Chapel Rd., Fuquay-Varina, NC 27526 USA

Name:_____ Title:_____

Company:_____

Shipping Address:_____

City:_____ State:_____ Postal/ Zip:_____

Billing Address:_____

City:_____ State:_____ Postal/ Zip_____

Telephone:_____ Fax:_____

Email:_____

Payment (select): VISA ____ AMEX ____ MC ____ Check ____

Credit Card #:_____ Expiration Date:_____

Exact Name on Card:_____

Qty.	Product ID	ISBN	Title	Price Ea	Total
Book Total:					
Sales Tax (North Carolina Residents please add 7% sales tax)					
Shipping: $5 per book in the USA, $10 per book outside USA (most countries). Lower shipping and rates may be available online.					
Total order:					

For a complete list please visit
www.AlthosBooks.com